COMMUNITY · CONNECTION

HOW DO THEY HELP?
UNITED WAY
BY KATIE MARSICO

CHERRY
LAKE
Publishing

Published in the United States of America by Cherry Lake Publishing
Ann Arbor, Michigan
www.cherrylakepublishing.com

Content Adviser: Rob Fischer, Ph.D., Professor and Director, Master of Nonprofit
Organizations, Jack, Joseph, and Morton Mandel School of Applied Social Sciences,
Case Western Reserve University
Reading Adviser: Marla Conn MS, Ed., Literacy specialist, Read-Ability, Inc.

Photo Credits: © Eff1708 | Dreamstime.com - Asian School Group In Uniform Playing
With Camera Photo, cover, 1, 21; © Sabphoto/Shutterstock, 5; © Eff1708 |
Dreamstime.com - Asian School Girl In Uniform Hold A Note Book In Her Arm Photo, 7;
© Photos.com/Thinkstock, 9; © Andre Jenny / Alamy Stock Photo, 11;
© Thinkstock Images/Thinkstock, 13; © Sjors737 | Dreamstime.com - Teacher Helping Pupil
Writing On Chalkboard Photo, 15; © Susan Chiang/istock, 17; © Steve Debenport/istock, 19

LIBRARY OF CONGRESS CATALOGING-IN-PUBLICATION DATA
Names: Marsico, Katie, 1980- author.
Title: United Way / by Katie Marsico.
Description: Ann Arbor : Cherry Lake Publishing, 2016. | Series: Community
  connections: how do they help? | Audience: K to Grade 3. | Includes
  bibliographical references and index.
Identifiers: LCCN 2015048735| ISBN 9781634710541 (hardcover) | ISBN
  9781634711531 (pdf) | ISBN 9781634712521 (pbk.) | ISBN 9781634713511
  (ebook)
Subjects: LCSH: United Way—Juvenile literature. | Charities—Juvenile
  literature.
Classification: LCC HV40 .M386 2016 | DDC 361.8—dc23
LC record available at http://lccn.loc.gov/2015048735

Cherry Lake Publishing would like to acknowledge the
work of The Partnership for 21st Century Learning.
Please visit www.p21.org for more information.

Printed in the United States of America
Corporate Graphics
CLFA11

UNITED WAY

CONTENTS

HOW DO THEY HELP?

CREATING STRONGER COMMUNITIES

In Ottawa—Canada's southeastern capital—roughly 1,400 young people are homeless. Life on the streets is dangerous and presents many challenges. One is receiving proper health care. Another is getting an education and finding work.

Fortunately, United Way funds programming to provide Ottawa's homeless youth with housing and job

Homelessness is one of the most widespread problems in North America.

Think about what it would be like to live on the streets. How do you think homeless people find food? Where do you think they sleep? Think about how challenging it must be for homeless children to do homework or even attend school!

5

opportunities. This **nonprofit** organization helps communities around the world address issues such as **poverty**.

United Way is active in more than 40 countries and territories. It strengthens communities by encouraging people to join forces. Together, residents build financial **stability** and tackle unemployment and homelessness. United Way makes it easier for people to receive an education and improve their health and well-being.

Having a strong education is a good foundation for success.

Are you able to guess how United Way creates educational opportunities in different communities? (Hint: One example involves constructing schools. United Way volunteers recently helped build 600 classrooms in the Philippines!)

FROM 1887 ONWARD

United Way programming traces back to Denver, Colorado. In 1887, Denver's population was booming. As it grew, so did issues such as poverty and a lack of health care.

Some of Denver's religious leaders realized they could help more people by working together. They formed a group to coordinate **social services**. They raised money for Denver's many different charities.

This cartoon shows some of the hardships Americans faced in the 1880s.

Apart from poverty, what welfare issues did people struggle with in Denver in the late 1800s? What specific health care problems existed? Did all children attend school? Search online or at the library for answers to these and other questions!

The movement in Denver became a model for other North American cities. People created Community Chests, which were groups that **monitored** welfare issues affecting specific communities. Community Chests involved volunteers who represented local charities, businesses, and social service agencies. They united to raise money, collect donations, and plan projects that helped improve residents' lives. In the early 1960s, such efforts were often described as "United Way" programming.

United Way supports their programs through donations from businesses—and people like you!

% 50% 60% 70% 80% 9

United Way ™

d Way of Greater Williamsburg

AL $1,550,1

Think about *your* experiences with teamwork in your own community. Did you find working with other people more effective than working alone? What are the possible advantages of different individuals and groups working together to improve social welfare?

Today, United Way Worldwide is headquartered in Alexandria, Virginia. This group oversees United Way organizations that strengthen communities around the globe. Every year, United Way programs aid roughly 50 million people.

For example, in Vadodara, India, United Way helps senior citizens pay their phone, electric, and gas bills. Meanwhile, programming in Atlanta, Georgia, provides 25,000 residents with health care services.

United Way creates programs that help everyone, from the youngest children to senior citizens.

LOOK!

Look online or at the library for images of United Way volunteers in action. What are they doing? How are their efforts helping to strengthen or improve each particular community shown?

13

It takes a wide variety of people to bring positive changes to so many lives. In order to build stronger communities, United Way relies on both paid staff and volunteers. They include doctors, **counselors**, lawyers, accountants, and teachers.

United Way depends heavily on people and organizations with strong financial, communication, and **management** skills. They coordinate the efforts of different individuals and groups involved in community projects.

Teachers have important skills that help United Way. Many teachers volunteer for United Way.

MAKE A GUESS!

Are you able to guess how many volunteers support United Way programs worldwide? If your guess was more than 2 million, you're right! United Way depends on 2.6 million volunteers. It also receives the help of 9.6 million donors.

POWERFUL PROGRAMMING

There are countless United Way programs that improve community welfare. Some are classes where instructors offer tips on how to be responsible with money. Others feature job training and guidance for people who are searching for work. In certain cases, United Way funding aids individuals and

Job training helps people find more rewarding careers.

Does United Way offer programming in your area? Are you familiar with any of the people or groups involved? What are their specific goals? Ask community leaders for answers to these and other questions!

17

families who are struggling financially or experiencing homelessness.

United Way helps people get and stay healthy, too. Efforts to achieve this goal include building hospitals and medical centers in areas that lack quality health care. Volunteers also teach residents the value of exercise and eating a balanced diet. In some communities, United Way provides healthy meals to children who don't have regular access to nutritious food.

Fruits and vegetables are an important part of a healthy diet.

LOOK!

Look online or at a library or medical center to find information on healthy eating. Then look at your own diet. Is it balanced? How do you think issues such as poverty affect nutrition?

Finally, thanks to United Way, people of all ages have more opportunities to learn and grow. Some volunteers show parents how to encourage their babies to communicate. Others help children develop reading skills or tutor students at risk of dropping out of school.

United Way shows that, when people work together, they spark powerful changes. Such changes improve individual lives and entire communities.

United Way helps children and families all over the world!

Show what making a difference looks like! Fold a piece of poster board in half. Label one side "Before" and the other "After." Then create drawings of different communities around the world both before and after United Way programming.

GLOSSARY

counselors (KOUN-suh-lurz) people trained to offer guidance on solving various personal and social problems

management (MAN-ij-muhnt) the process of dealing with or controlling things or people

monitored (MAH-nih-tuhrd) observed and tracked the progress or quality of something

nonprofit (nahn-PRAH-fit) not existing for the main purpose of earning more money than is spent

poverty (PAH-vur-tee) the state of being poor

social services (SO-shuhl SUR-vis-iz) programming that benefits a community in areas such as housing, education, and health care

stability (stuh-BIL-ih-tee) the state of being secure and unlikely to change suddenly or unexpectedly

welfare (WEL-fair) the happiness, health, and well-being of an individual or group

FIND OUT MORE

BOOKS

Ancona, George. *Can We Help? Kids Volunteering to Help Their Community*. Somerville, MA: Candlewick Press, 2015.

Cohn, Jessica. *Improving Communities*. Huntington Beach, CA: Teacher Created Materials, 2013.

Senker, Cath. *Poverty and Hunger*. Mankato, MN: Smart Apple Media, 2012.

WEB SITES

KidsHealth—Be a Volunteer!
kidshealth.org/kid/feeling/thought/volunteering.html
Read about different ways to volunteer in your community, as well as the benefits of helping others.

United Way Worldwide
www.unitedway.org
Learn more about the history of United Way and the latest news on current programming.

INDEX

ABOUT THE AUTHOR

Katie Marsico is the author of more than 200 children's books. She lives in a suburb of Chicago, Illinois, with her husband and children.

24